Slut

Slut

poetry by

Atif Shahjad

Published
from Dhaka, Bangladesh
1st Edition
First published on 2022

Copyright © 2022
by
Atif Shahjad

ISBN: 979-8361803644

Social
Twitter/@atifshahjad
Facebook/@Shahjedatif
Instagram/@atif_shahjad
Tumblr/@atifshahjad

Email
atifshajed67@gmail.com

Dedicated

A girl I meet at my friend's party.

You're not a slut, Mira.
You're just going through life
how life is taking you there.
Just like me.
Because If you're a slut, who isn't a slut.
So be well.

Contents

Blueberry lips

I want my soul to be touched
by the tip of your hands.
I want roe dawn to come,
out of that room,
divided,
different people,
days aftermath,
allow the moment to hold my softback.
When night comes,
that share bad will be wet by our sweat,
greenlight will remind us if you can see,
how dare you not have me.
I always needed your youngness
when that hand drafts my shore,
wind cries out loud,
lusted word screamed,
bluebird in my heart,
stops short when the mindset of love runs out.
I wanted my soul to exist
to be touched
when this skin had
what indeed unseen,
feeling that carry,
every sea I chase,
a tree that I buried,
awaken gazelle to run,
hunger for greening weed,
I am that soft meat

waiting for your bitter flame,

for a simple touch on my soul.

I want nothing in everything

when your hand clams my soul,

I want those wet lips between my lips,

unrestricted heartfelt moment

that makes me feel loved.

What a wish I dream

you that come when

there is a tumble within,

I want that touch on my shielded heart,

by you, only your lips and softened love.

by atif shahjad

Blue film

Black is better than blank.
Wash your hands and open your body.
Let's go to the washroom with the blue picture in hand,
beautiful breasts, the scent of that body, the lustful inner thought, the
body pulls, soft love gets out.
Everyone knows what a blue picture is,
so get ready
to take forever.
I see blue pictures
when the hand is busy,
to rub the little black mamba,
that spot, private part,
the weight of the buttocks sticks,
the mango bar between two legs,
when the nunu, dudu, balls, ring-ting—the blue films mean and
beautiful sex scenes come to my intellect, fantasizing, replaying,
what're you doing, watching me perform the secret ritual...

Woman needler

Stage man
stays lone
fucks at home,
while those
who is the mistress
of man,
stays far away at their sweet home.
Because money makes sunny day bloom.
Many women want,
what no one gives,
then the money is here,
opening up a path
like she wants a glimpse of us,
when she is right outside,
in her mind,
she wants to fall for the human touch.
So come and please me,
what no one does to me.
No one,
the husband,
the lover of another,
the creep,
new old lover,
the true admirer,
all don't go far.
One who does,
that one
does not give a fuck.

by atif shahjad

Here I want everything,

where passing time in someone's arms,

isn't so bad.

That's why I make one call right now.

You small or new,

come to mama.

Here are boxes of money waiting.

Please me.

Take it.

Come again,

to grain another lust in my joy

when I call.

Lust is your threshold

in many conditions,

have to please me

deep inside my holes,

that is your goal

to please me,

in every way, I say so.

You need to be the bad boy,

all left behind,

mine,

and your truth is me.

So do you need me now,

then come to mama,

and see what I can be.

You have beautiful lips.

I say it to her many times,

her kiss was so tantalizing.

But I wonder what will you do

if I show you what ask if you will do,

after feeling exhilarating

when you and I will have each of our joy

into our wet lips, wide into our mouth, touch and lovelessness,

deeper inside,

simultaneously,

drinking from the taste of our skin,

hmm, won't you like it?

You will think to keep your dignity,

as I will, but we will know,

it will be the thing

that we will not have any more space between us

When you and I will be mated again and again.

Because without thinking of you,

yesterday, today, next day will not pass away.

—what else

by atif shahjad

She dying hard for a blow

I saw you eyeing me for so long.
Would you care nothing to taste it ...?
Then, make your coin flip,
did you see the winning chip—
In bed, you and I were mumbling, grumbling, tumbling,
what would be the word when your hand took my body in his ash,
I liked it.
Lips pouring you milk and honey,
two women, one hidden inside,
one outside making that mistake of sex,
rising and tapping her front, ride you,
oh god, go slow.
You're loving me the way you please,
Still that way I made myself enjoy.
Not the first scream you left inner rhythm.
Lipstick pours your summer inside the mouth.
Then again, I let it rise on a day,
ready for the second round,
take it from behind.
Yet your honey bee didn't chase my bunny.

Arousal

Object to forget the old smell, but ready to go.
I fuck someone with money,
while the mind does not have sex.
At the time of death,
at the moment, if there is a spider around,
quality cries out in the skin of both,
fool provokes the treasure of the lustful root
like you need only one closing punctuation.
If injured,
what a wonderful wake-up call, happiness.
Black spots, fur cover, red lipstick,
everyone knows,
when he wakes up, he becomes a man,
oh-hu-ahu or ah ahh,
I rub my hands,
softly bite her neck,
I kiss her with my lips together.
Lost inside, ah, what happiness I'm feeling...
Naked, two hands extended forward,
arousal goes on,
until the next phase has gone.

by atif shahjad

Mistake or moonlight

Was the need to be needed inside her was I needed—then why did
my lion make me go wild in my sane mind?
I say it often like it's a mistake, but is it?
I did desire it,
I wanted to swim in her womanhood.
That's why I got myself naked
and jumped onto her naked body.

Blue skin

Day and night, I watch you, sec, minutes, hours, days,
what are you doing, who's with you...?
I imagine scenes where you and I'll be together forever,
wanted relations have to ensure.
Whoever will make you for her, friends you sit and chat with,
I will concern myself to make you take distance.
Then I will appear in front of you.
You will fall for my beauty, drown in my kind caring love.
My soft-innocent eye will tell you to protect me.
The stillness I will hold will empower you,
and you will want that control over me more and more.
My perfect boobs and ass will be the thing you will not avoid in bed.
My fake orgasm and satisfied body move will make you like me and
love me madly.
I will be there for you, making everything you want to construct from
your point of view.
I will keep tabs on you, make you my little play dog while being your
puppy love.
Whatever I will see fit, it has to be done by you,
or I will get upset.
Yet I will manipulate you.
So don't even look at other women. If you do, they will die.
From time to time, I will have some friends with befits.
Despite your suspicion will not come up with any cost.
Because I am your wanted warden for the happy home you made in
your mind.
While I stay awake, you will be all mine, every inch.

by atif shahjad

All of the worst is the outcome of our best's

They work together for one night,

cohabitation is under investigation,

the man had never seen the girl before,

but her body was bought instead of the specified money.

The bell rings, take it, hump jump push fuck as you wish,

then the meaning of it will fly, who will be happy...

The dove is ready to push inside herself,

for whom who bought the sunny days glory.

Give money, take the body, but gently,

the girl is also human.

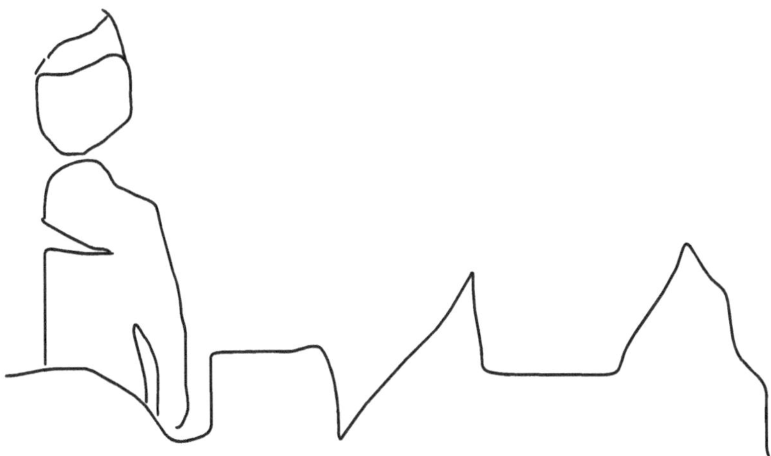

It was a wedding
when I saw her in her wedding dress,
keeping close to that freshness, I was amazed.
Her laugh was the best thing I didn't get to capture.
That glory gate awaits when I knew,
I wanted her, to make mine, only to keep.
Then I saw her taking another man
when I broke my heart again.
For the remorse, for a few minutes,
I cried as she made out with another shining knight.
Then I congratulate them,
went back to my chair,
eat like a manic who just got released from jail.
Again, I fell in love.
I saw her talking to her friend,
in a sleeveless dress, beauty, and fearless body.
I wanted that taste when I have gone to her,
I knew what I will have in bed.
Then when her husband came to take her away,
again, my heart broke.
Every while later, I fall,
love will steer my little heart,
I want, I do, I get my ecstasy,
so display I don't fall in love
because I fall in love many times, many ways.

—I fall many times

by atif shahjad

Now new job names for men can be heard

Sold out their exchanges.
However, many things are individual,
young boy, the price is high,
muscular, somewhat handsome, fit middle-aged or young stud,
demand is among their women.
There was a lot of gossip between them,
who can take it longer, do step how—

You know, man, you're not a coward.
That's why I will shoot cannons to kill,
right-their little left,
do right,
take pride, kill sex mosquitoes on demand of money.

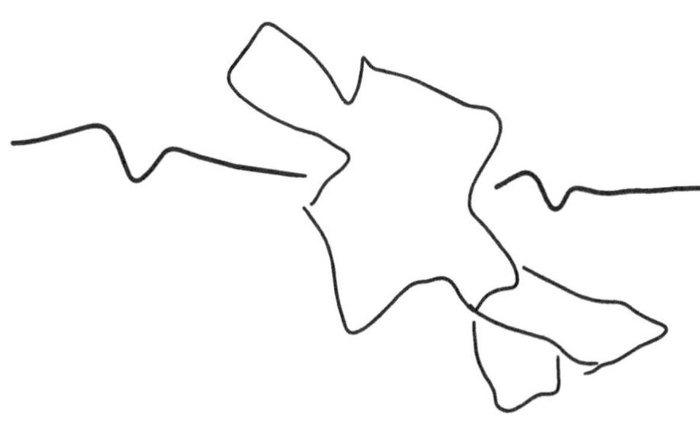

Every picture you took of my body,
I wish that eye would have me that way
when every picture sinks a long-lasted moment.

—*photographs*

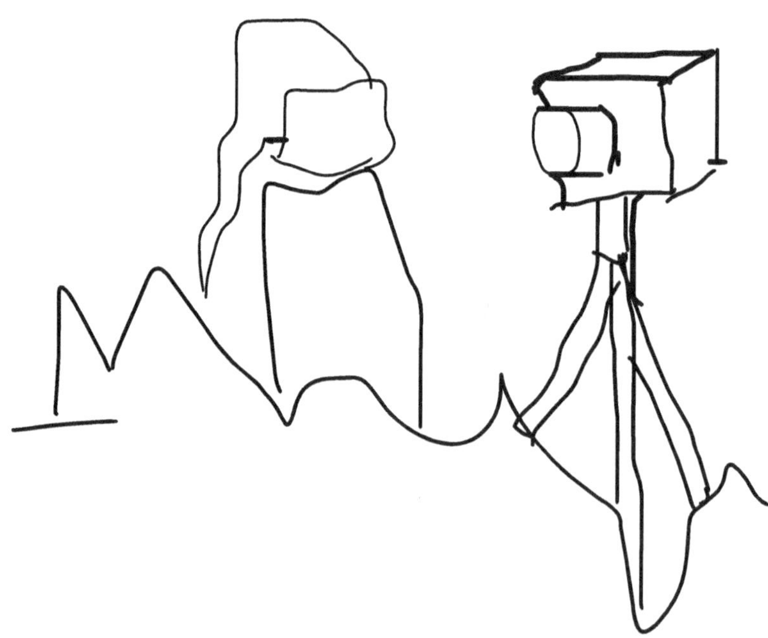

by atif shahjad

Dark desire

The day I have seen you naked,
you opened up my skirt.
Your hand touching my neck
when your lips said,
I will not say no if you have me,
I have been hungry for a long time.

You moved your body softly through my skin.
I felt it, like the horizon of every sea within me
in every possible way.
We had that joy when you kissed me,
going deep inside me.
Desire moves my body slowly
as my heart stopped there to say,
I loathsome all of it, but still yearned for you
when you enter in back and hit my colon,
I hold myself to have that pleasure
as your hand rubs my boobies.

After that time,
I wish your warm body to stay
in my arms, cooling off,
wet lip inside my mouth.

The day we slept together

That's enough, is not it...?
For a few hours, night stayed young,
what a pussy, what a body,
just the meatloaf to eat,
wondering ...

That night came after many months after we met,
now it's all honeymoon.
She moved her pillow,
laid down on the bed upside down
on his cook,
it's nice to feel the skin.
My left hand was on her neck,
massaging her – Oh-hmm-s, mmm, had gone out, muttering,
it was like two different persons
just met as a stranger,
but fail to enclose ourselves,
he tried oneself best,
she is pleased to feel;
both were feeling each other,
traveling to discover real love.

It's just one of those nights
when two lovers have fallen deeper into each other.
Then that naughty look, smiling, or direct-action reply.
They take each other.
Before he tried, she undresses her upper nighty,
blouse,

see it, his dwelling feeling fallen into his desire,
they kiss each other,
she was given her away to him, willingly.
He graded her down, front;
slowly his penis hits the ground.
Her clitoris was rubbing by his waist and body,
right then, she had an obsessive orgasm.
Then his thunder enters inside
after that hurt comes a little.
She wanted him deep inside her,
while later, he stands up straight,
looked at her to do what she has - as walking in the porn world has
shown us,
have women give you roughy blow—
But her pride sees it as ugliness
to blow the manhood out of him.
Then he has gone to please her,
got both hands raised high, to them self-comfort each other's
warmness.
Then she uncomfortably put it,
tasted, and he was in his heaven.
Then her hair covers her face,
he backs it and took her in his arms,
on his stand lap,
he is kissing from back,
when junior enters from behind her glorious joy.
Then in bed, they stayed,
had each other how they wanted,
until the man had enough to himself
and women can have an hour-long organism.

That night not grown in distance, they laid into each,
midnight,
she and he were stunning.
He slept slowly, she quickly.
Morning,
they share laughter, tea.
When she was standing over the balcony,
he stands behind her
touching her round butt,
rubbing her belly and chest,
hug her
when his hard cook was feeling her behind,
she said, what are you up to now;
ha-ha, hey, you are pitching me.
Then he whispers into her ear, bite it, softly,
they laugh oddly, lustful,
then they fell into a kiss.

That night was our first.
It just sought of came up into us,
shown how much she was wild,
he was pitchy.
After that night,
many nights came,
not like this anymore.
Yet wonder stay in the mirror.
Why did we have sex that night;
fixation of the body made dark humor!
We were, had it all alone,

yet many thoughts came out as a mistake.

But it happened,

every feeling that stood,

she has taken him as he flamed her within himself,

postman was waiting to collect.

We collect within itself,

two bodies;

made love,

sin that slept and laid behind,

made peace in joy within each selfless phase of the body.

That first touch of his, her soft feeling lips ... Dripping and tripping on

sells on lustful desire,

to play.

And we did ... so long, so beautiful.

To be honest, I fantasize about him more often,

how would it feel when he will be inside me?

As his unrequited lover,

whenever I see him

I wanted to jump onto him.

So I had.

In the dream, my boyfriend said,

don't be rude for today

that you're my breakfast and dinner

when I have never been given into the way of special treatment.

As I'm with him, saying to him when the mouth is all around his wet banner,

I waited a long time; do you like this ...

But it didn't get out of hand, for a few times we did have that long time meeting,

until my love got left out,

that stayed scent of secret.

—lone fantasy of my unrequited love

by atif shahjad

Mister and Miss

It's always the innocent-looking one
who is the wild one.
That glass they wear,
it shows much illimitable game
when her hand keeps wondering,
his hand gets what that day wants.
All the saying,
why the delays,
I want to see how that wicked touch will cry,
two bodies stood there, sinful,
until their greediness comes to them.

That body of ours,
take chance with compassion.
He cares about it
when his cooks stand to listen.
She provoked uncertain attitudes and hers,
her woman's part is also the same.
Ashamed you, can't even look at your own vagina.
Sometimes brains stay in those branded scars,
to defeat, the wordless winning.
Like me, can't even think about love without my dick.

—only then

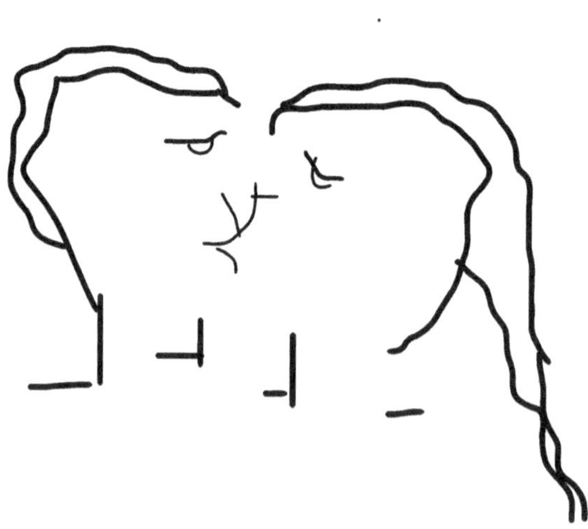

by atif shahjad

Unaccounted

Do you wanna stay over tonight—
He and she was bathing together,
he asked her without knowing
because in classifying bitchy acts underneath,
she is a married and unsatisfied woman.
Again, she doesn't wish
because she just had a fling.
After that,
no man ever asked her that
like
after having casual sex in an art gallery basement.

It started,
I don't want the coffee.
Then why don't we skip it?

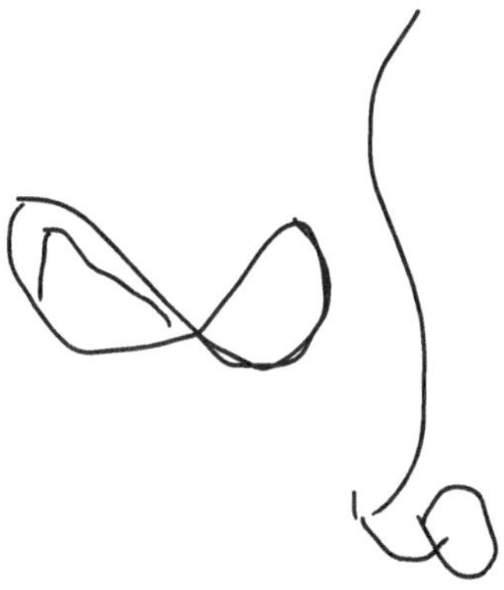

It's a compulsive reality

It's better not to know with whom whose bed I'm sleeping.
Next edition, we kiss, we get close,
then it just happened.
Then we both went our different ways,
where we will never meet.

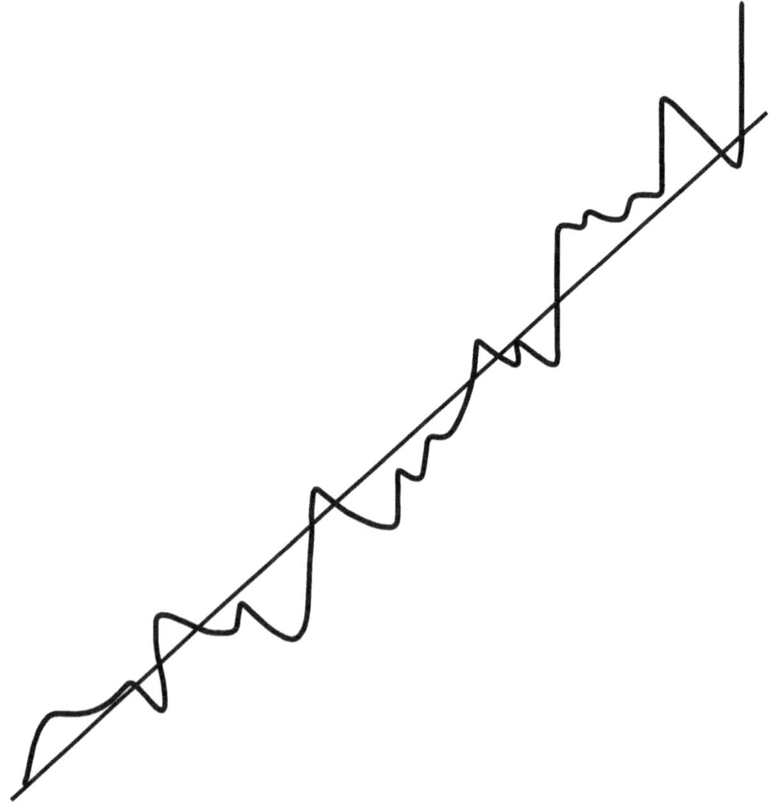

by atif shahjad

When we love, we want bitterness.

But when that flame of bitterness turns into love,

it became something different.

Where it's better to live as it was.

So, loving that person was not the wrong thing I did.

The wrong I did was,

thought it will easy.

Despite understanding, I wanted that bitterness of you,

which for a little while made my love whole for you and me.

—your bitter pumpkin within you

Ultimate woman

She is not the she.

In her mother's womb, she was born as me.

That me stayed long as she.

Inside her, a man is sleeping.

After a time, she changed.

The sailing tale, on puppy dog nail.

All of her is there, yet not there to break.

In her everything, all is pure estrogen.

This perfect beautiful woman is a man.

All this you see, the perfect diamond on your body.

All this is because your she, your he, you're both left to be.

Breathing not so quiet as the deep sea.

One body, two souls, dancing in the dark.

Now comes to question the foul goal of destiny.

Who can be, who can I see?

All there is left to know, she is not the she.

by atif shahjad

Daddy issues

I have given everything I had.

Still, you left us, dad.

Mom cried many nights

because your self-loathing manhood took her pride.

And I was just nine years old,

living in myself, in my room, with no friends to cope with.

At age sixteen, I got pregnant.

Not because I wanted,

it just happened.

But I killed that parasite without much thinking

because it's broken what my childhood hour mostly fears.

At age twenty, I already slept with many boys, young and older men

you can count,

taken all kinds of creepy drugs,

done things to get by in life.

But sex was my escape

because for those moments alone,

they wanted nothing and everything.

And you, yet nothing at all.

Irony can so painful,

just like having fresh start can be true.

The body of compassion

This is their policy when they shatter in front of you.
That's the decent thing to do,
and it should end there
without making it the nonsense you like to see.
Want or not, like to go home with me - when that girl on the street
says it out loud,
sir unlocked his wallet,
while broker says as you want, as you wish, so here it is.
Just remember what else there can be.

I saw her that day.
She was lying on the bed with oiled curtains and stains.
Her legs are crippled, yet not her body, she was a beauty.
Her body was also sold at auction between these four walls
when men leave their semen inside her.
No matter what condition it is, she lays down, with her legs open,
calling all the world gentleman to her comar-taj.
Various men unbuttoned their pants, listening to their little boss
without consideration.

This time, everyone's words came much later
when all they want is an acknowledged relief.
Hour after hour comes many new men.
The girl does not have to do anything but stay in bed.
Call, take her, and enjoy throwing dirt in this dustbin.
Won't you like fuck my brains out, sir?
Then, the prudent conscience says, in whose favor is your truth.

by atif shahjad

In the end, she's nothing but a whore, who understand well how can
she give less, how can she take more,
but not know how to disobey.
Alive she is, she was born to make this reality, nor I dare to say,
what can a girl on red street be born to do?

Age is not more than that,
the bird that has been running since eleven, selling its chastity to the
owner,
before looking, not looking back.
Masculinity wants to dig all the holes, so they do in that bird.
But one day, a teenager arrived at the end of her youth.
When he saw that, the brokers opened the faction and told him only
about money.
If there are ashes, you will get it, whether you want it or a beautiful
girl, it will take more water like an extrovert who likes to be alone with
his prey.

Then he entered the room, no mercy sat, he posed,
the beauty I wanted - the crippled prostitute without her folklore.
He wanted her because its price was low, and sympathy intercourse
happened to be hardcore, more than that, he can relate.
Because that's how he thinks of a human being.
Ten bodies come to him in the dark of night, sit down, eat, and get
what they want,
then get used to every fun because he can't run.
Chit will take everything for what you exchange, roaming in this
blankness, he is whore just like her.
Whatever the other body wants to do,
this happiness of arrow and body is not found anywhere else.

So the young man understood.
Yet why couldn't he touch her
the way that everyone did.
When the girl sees this stem of his, running to her in search of
something, she says,
what, I don't want to understand.
You can take happiness as you want, this body is mature.
The price of a lip kiss will not be on your lips.
What do you want, this wet saliva cave on your penis,
feeling happy, don't want it now?
Then be like the million men who come to accept, don't be different.

by atif shahjad

One right now

I see the glimpse of us,
where you have the golden egg.
Maybe that is why many flies come by.
A few pennies rang to get her.
Did understand why three-quarters of the whole body is not clothed
because she was posing for somebody, everybody.
Therefore, his custom goes on,
body worship or body skeleton, that young man of religion,
booking her, looking at more but in binding conscience.
The woman's vagina is thrilling, so he wants to experience it.
Now he is not a man.
The breasts and buttocks of a half-naked woman in front of him are
pulling him,
yet some are taking time off to think, just like he did,
telling himself, God, forgive my one last sin.

Gently they beat slowly
were you the asshole one,
want to get the pleasure of being young,
wanting to flesh your semen in other people's bodies, nothing more,
even when the skinny underaged girl is on the job.
No, seeing that, the girl calls him with all her might,
smooches his body parts, her genitals give pleasure to the face, yet
she responds to it do what was the kid you wanted to experience,
every time you cum all over her body...
Because she gets to left empty-handed,
but he can't accomplish the same.

After a while, the boy showed kindness to the girl,

sitting behind her and telling stories,

which was not old for the girl, one in ten.

But most of the time, they escape.

At least their wild form comes and changes

when everything inside and outside of this body is squeezed,

accused of harassment, and the anal sex takes a hint of new

happiness.

Someone plays with new bad habits, and toys again.

In the imagination, the girl transforms all the disabilities into play.

by atif shahjad

Arani

For dear girl Arani,

the young boy had a bright green heart, eager to know all.

The girl also said what he wanted to hear.

But the boy did not return the glory for using the girl's body.

Then why take it, it did not wake up in question.

She was lying on that bed with sores.

She looked beautiful with her medium breasts,

and the idea of rubbing one's own happiness was enough.

What bullshit Arani believes,

I'm getting high thinking about all of it.

But the girl knows that the young man will come again.

At the age of eighteen, I know this luxury impresses me.

Everybody is falling in love right, so let me fall.

What is love if that is all

fuck and tell, go and ring a bell ...

But she said, do treat my love like a habit.

Then you will find a man beside a beautiful young girl.

where the money is very old,

combatting in the so-called broker court.

A few evenings later, these wild hands are warming up in the

company of that young girl Arani.

Foolish may many thinks, dear girl Arani,

you see, all is not what it seems to be …

Love isn't a money sign or pickup line,

it's just a sinking feeling.

But you think, sex will make it happen.

Can you tell if it does?

Then Inner's story is supplied to the people,

the wind blows,

when two lags hear the call,

you are a beggar, a swear word,

then semen remains in the vagina between them.

You don't have to wipe your clothes every time,

but no one stops, do they?

In this game,

houses, smoking pots, cars go everywhere under the trees.

where the broker is Mr. Sagared himself, that young bird.

Everyone eats, but only if they can take it,

where appreciating is not beautiful, but beautiful diamonds in price.

This girl Arani is happy behind the giant, that boy, the first one, and many more to come.

So he takes, just as her honey and milk, so is happiness,

and goes far from her to kill her attachment disease.

While she thinks, its something more.

by atif shahjad

After sex

9.23 am, closed-door priests
say,
it's an evil thing we have done.
00.00 clock, God says,
to have each bodies euphoria
who made them the edge to decay,
women on the bad,
man on his naked shore,
sea had to go,
meet their happiest years.
House woman says
it's what pigs want in their ugly furry.
Lover knows that sweet sorrow brightness of human
sugar on top and sweet cherry.
9.30 am last night was an unforced error of love,
it will not be forgotten.

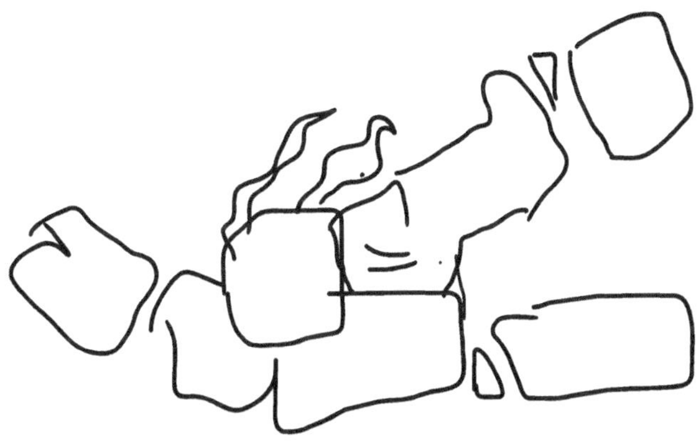

Round is the question

Oh, my god, I thought it would be beautiful
when we will cum together.
But all seems slow and rusty desire between two people - trying to
polish their sex drive
when many times they wanted to have two satisfying orgasms, they
just can't
at the same time.

by atif shahjad

When a sad virgin boy makes themselves a man

Like many obsessions with compassion and need,
that young man returned, but this time there was no more fear.
Take off your clothes and have sex like an animal.
Out of pity, he took his penis all the way.
The previous young man was not even seen while leaving, seen as a
boy searching to be replaced, and he was.
Because after many ends, the girl he met to be a man, knew what
power she holds over them, as they hold over themselves while they
change, growing as men, taking a lovemaking test.
She is now alive, breathing, accepted him, ho or innocent, who gives
a fuck, where he saw numerous gifts in him, after fucking the girl
again and again.
And that's what ensues
when a sad virgin boy makes themselves a man while humping.

Me and my wife and her

One day, a few months back,
I understood she loved me.
But a few minutes after, I look back to this day,
said I'm a dick who did listen to his dick
because my wife's sister fell in love with me,
even though I'm married,
I just went into her to make a home run.

We are sitting on the sofa,
watching a movie, it was freezing winter cold,
me and my wife were under the same blanket,
embracing each other,
I'm feeling her breast, rubbing her neck and back.
And on the other corner sofa, my wife's sister is sitting next to us.
I know she can understand what both of us are doing under the
blanket.
But the way she looked at me, she adores
and me for loving her sister.
Soon, I understand from the vibe
that she would respond to any desire
if I showed the same care for her.
But I calm myself, telling myself to be quiet, pervert.
I said to myself, again and again,
it's not right, it's not right,
while this heart of mine wanted it more than my faith.
After that day, it began.
She used to give signals, wearing tights clothes, talking sweets
whenever she is here

when I am in the house,

she used to change clothes

without shutting the door.

Knowing I will know, I will see her in the corner of my eye.

I also did the same, flirting, taking kinda dirty,

like I'm talking to a stranger whom I like to make my lover.

And one day, it got out the red line

when I wanted to fuck her, make sweet love to her, fuck her young

body, smell her, embrace her intimately.

But instead, I said, let's talk. And understand what I am saying.

What the hell is wrong with me?

Why did I say that?

Because next month I found out my wife was having an affair.

And the reason she told me when I asked her why

it's because I was obsessive about loving her all the time

when I'm loving her.

Because all the time I'm loving her!

That's even a reason!

She felt caged in a boxed room because of my love.

It's supposed to be the other way around.

Love is supposed to be the done deal

where I just wanted to be part of your symphony,

so hold on tight, don't let go.

That's the rule we suppose to follow.

Is it really that wrong to love someone so obsessively by loving them

truly, honestly, faithfully, completely...?

And that day, I said to myself,

what a prude you are,

now both of them are gone.

Her raw naked love was showing

when the public eyes made her bosom

a minefield they wanted to throw themselves.

Her every lover did, had her everything.

Still, no one wait to see,

who is real she,

just like those eyes desire her naked love.

—*her longing*

by atif shahjad

A lot

He has a shard of doubt,
so he fucks himself with other people.
With what life he lives,
wish he could undo a lot.

You sneak into my room
when no one noticed,
we were in a hurry
for having sex,
kissing each other.
Then, someone you care about heard it.
I ask with my eye,
who the hell is there?
Come back after we finish.
Right then, I heard the knock-in our door.

—pick love

by atif shahjad

Hyphen

The sign hyphen is used to join words to combine meanings,
just like a man and woman makes a meaning
when they both get close.
To indicate the division of their own personality, feeling each other
naked, having sex was the humane conception we make for our
sake.
Whereas fucking each until our pleasure organ cries in tears,
is the end of a new beginning,
where how to go down on someone is the end of a line,
to indicate a missing or implied element
as in short and long-term.
It's complicated, I know.
Yet we try.
I try to feel all of it when the feeling of emptiness hits,
wanting to have someone takes the rush away.
Because you seek it, don't you?
Where it goes, he knows the desire, she knows the low,
I know how I wish to experience all of the above
when there is something interesting about all of us.
What—
The wine is singing. The bed is calling us. Then I have taken her,
whispering into her ears, when my one hand was rubbing her neck,
another got lost beneath her dress, telling her, show them, honey—
moistening the love and compassion into clay, boiling the urges of
lovemaking, just like the hyphen.

Secession bedtime story

Time days stopped
while she bagged in her heart,
wanting everything in sex, a real touch,
his manly part,
what can do one man and a woman,
while their aroused part falls.
Nowadays between us, everything let happening
when beauty-conscious wealth goes on poking,
woman's desire for satisfied vulnerability dies in other people's arms,
while sustaining her own self,
mind say choose what you would like to settle down,
every tool to make love
has to be tried, so he does, she takes, she wants, he obeys.
It feels good when each other mouths please other,
rubbing harshly into each other.
Then sleep or talk
when two people lay beside or sit with each other or do a thing,
while in their hearts,
that vague want of amusement going through the rooftop.
After sex, that time you spend,
create that handy work of touching and love, to have deep affection.
Because she is not unlike men, unlike so many women, she just
wants to love by human touch, not the vague response of love.

by atif shahjad

Then the wind claps the windows

My fantasy stopped.

God, who hell just broke nocturnal emission!

A little bit of time later,

I would have felt the edge.

And

little later,

the whole dream would have gotten pregnant.

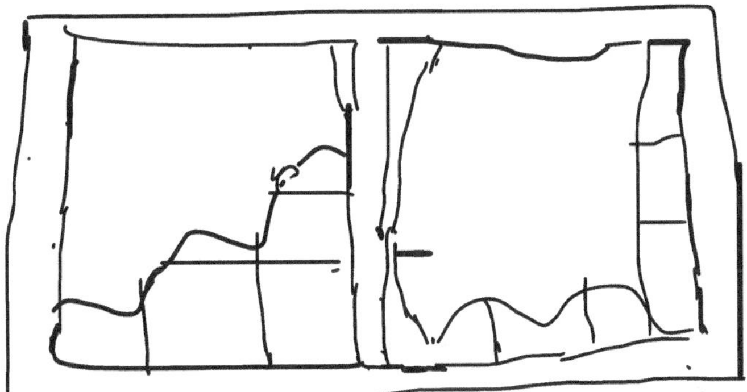

Story

It's getting late.
She is not picking up her phone.
We are getting married today.
What is she doing?

Tonight, a bride partying
like it's new year's eve.
It was her bachelor night fire.
So her friend took her outing to enjoy.
At early midnight, after their outing, they went to a bar.
They're having a good time, dancing, talking, laughing.
And funny enough,
there she got half drunk, just like her friends,
then in moments relapse, her friends dare her to flirt with a guy,
criticizing that she lost her muse, now that she is getting married.
So she did.
Later on, they got to talking,
while he saw himself fit to be her companion.
Then ridiculously enough,
he invited her to the apartment.
And she was gone with him,
half a drunk she is, wanting to get laid.
Hours later, her drunk friends went home without looking for her.
Thinking she is just drunk,
doing some shitty things on her own.
So they did not look to find and stay with the bride.
They're just lost in the fun.
Nonetheless, the night did not stop.

by atif shahjad

In the morning bride woke up in an unknown apartment,

she sees a guy

laying next to her, naked.

Then she remembers

last night's deed,

the restless sex,

even they enjoyed backdoor snooping,

which she never gave to her boyfriend in the last three years.

Now she feels guilty.

Today is her wedding day.

Everyone waiting,

and she runs to her home,

while in mind, one thing is clung, what have I done ...?

There she is.

I knew she won't have cold feet

because I love her.

Where are you been?

I called you numerous times, but you did not pick up.

You are supposed to be here at 10, now you are late.

Forget that, are you ready to get married?

He said all these things while she just stops in front of him,

thinking about her fault,

she was ready

to tell the truth.

But when he asked are you ready to get married

with a cute face, carrying a smile on his mouth,

she stops and looks at him.

Then lie to his face with a strange smile,
I dozed off because last night I slept late.
You know,
because of all the drinking and late-night parties.
That's why I was late.
And he looked at her unknowingly, then said,
ok, get ready.
Today is the big day.
Then said, you know that
I love you more than anything, right?
She said, yeah, I love you too.

by atif shahjad

She saw

Did you see that?

She has a huge block of tits.

Are those real!

Huge, you can see it raft around an ice cream stick,

you can do it again and again while feeling heavenly.

What?

Shut up, stupid...

Inner flame bugging, giving me thoughts to do things—

Thinking about her body is a deprived thing that cannot get out.

Even fantasying her gone rouge in seven spaces of lustful desire.

Next, her cheekbone, her decisive look, her chubby waist, sweaty

chest dripping in tenderness calling by my name

gave me an instant hard-on.

And funny enough, she saw it happen.

Came in front of my face with her huge block of boobies—

I can't breathe, I can't breathe.

Shut up, stupid.

I want those train wrecks.

Shut your screaming.

She will know.

Telling myself what you ice cream stick thinking,

while I'm thinking of her beauty, fascinated, aroused.

Whereas I am getting used to this,

yet never knew a heart could break itself

because I can't get those boobies for myself.

Yet I looked at those, hungry, imagining many things,

I want those oceans, those huge tits.

Careful what you wish not for

The day I came home from college,

I thought I'll be alone.

But my sister has someone over.

So I left with the last chapter,

what a loneliness tragedy I'm.

Then in the summertime,

I invited the present time, my soulmate.

She came to meet with the family.

One night my sister said

she saw her with a guy in our town bar.

I asked who,

she said who knows the truth.

Turns out,

he is her ex

my mom's forbidden sinner,

the one I saw with someone to feel loneliness tragedy.

Sometime after, I thought, Is it a hollywood rom-com or something?

What the fuck is wrong with me?

Then break up happened,

family separation ensued.

But then my ex went back to him.

That asshole!

Like all this never happened.

Months later, all that left,

refaced,

some event that would never be meant to happen,

if I was more careful...

by atif shahjad

Old evergreen flower, 1 loved you

Back then, you were a much older woman than me, but I loved you.

If it was the opposite case, that would have looked fine to everyone.

Because when you said I will get old when you'll be young,

I said, then I will love the older you.

You're the one whom I fantasized about, envied, and loved—

I don't know, it's love or dominance I wanted...

But in every dream, I had, it was you who... Never mind.

Why is that matter so much?

I saw an equal lover even when you used your older character to

avoid me, nasty sex habits.

While it was fun to play hard get, wasn't it?

We knew it won't work in the end,

made some high misreading.

But we stayed in touch, in present, in our little moments.

And sex in our dungeon was passionate.

Our uncommon love was_ I don't how to describe it.

Because you knew exactly what you wanted,

whereas I was a young man who just stepped out on the brave new

world.

You didn't want much but didn't give less.

Maybe for a little while.

But I loved you.

It was worth it all, all of it.

One day you broke it off, in your choice

Don't really know why?

You loved me in your own way.

And it broke for a time when you left.

A year later, you came back and wanted our misfit-overwhelming
relationship back.

Came to my home, drunk, sleep-deprived,

and said to me I missed you a lot.

You slept like a baby in my room.

But I moved on.

My love life newly began when you weren't there.

Next morning once again, you vanished—

That evening I went to your apartment.

See you are okay... But a little later, we are in bed together.

After that restless sex, we got into talking for hours.

But somehow, it felt like I was there but not really there anymore.

In the time we were together,

I asked, why did you break it off?

And why do you think you want me back?

You explained you expected something that I wasn't.

Like I wanted something that you aren't.

But still, I didn't get what was wrong I didn't see!

For three days,

I stayed in with you in your apartment, all by ourselves.

But at last, we ended it.

I loved you, still do someway—

That's why I wanted you with all of my heart, with all of your
unbearable complexity.

But a lasting painful song was playing in my head.

If I look back, go back to you just for a bit—will I breathe twice.

So walked out and left.

And you just sat on the couch, watching me walk out.

by atif shahjad

Other people

When he betrayed the one in his life,

he lost in that cost.

When another woman's desire became his,

he fought to lose the older one.

So he thinks, for him, beloved goddesses are arguing.

Still, her body doesn't taste good

as another woman does.

Then why have her in the first place?

Namedrop

A rumor made me live in a hellish room,

dying breadfruit rotten in this tree

whenever reason comes, god appears to see.

But my god never showed up to me,

as that lie tied my life on all the other sides,

being careful, taking a lot of leaves of faith.

Yet years try, all got in the monster fire,

as it has taken my everything,

I left nothing to hold.

Dealing with my feelings,

the teacup was broken on the floor,

altar glass pieces slashing my soul,

I ask, why did that half-truth become my life?

End and early, everything shuts down, rotting life,

so I took that only relief

where I can hide in my own disbelief.

by atif shahjad

Companion

That day I saw a man go from invisible to real,
A piece of love survived in the last room that lasted lust
when suddenly learned to walk the path of utopia accompanied by
his attraction.
The companion you, residence grows inferiority in that lonely heart,
fear if you let him be separated, all loss cannot go away.
Because this path is covered in many broken glasses.
Yet the greatest love appears in the music of lustful sex.
And that is he taken, what many cannot see broken,
I want my partner besides my own hot skin, in a hint of longing,
in longing he made him real what seem so invisible.

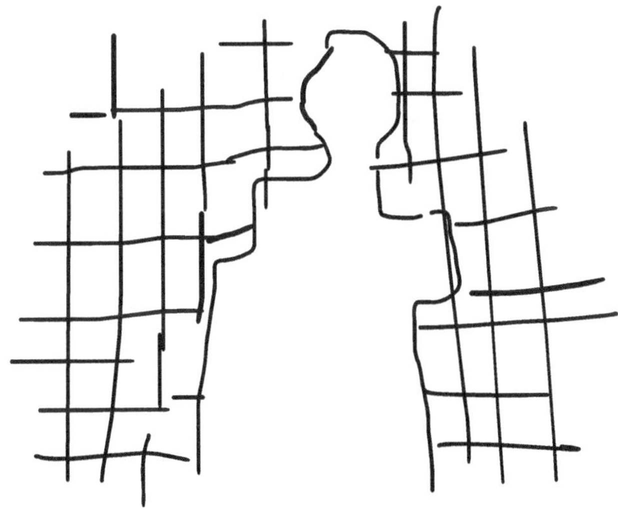

Peep

A touch of the hand makes my body unknown,

my lip, my heart, my everything down on the sun.

When I woke late Tuesday, our time went by.

Meet me again, making that wish was a foolish try.

Life part top, sexual knock on the body,

don't get lazy to do it again and again like a donkey.

Believing for both of us,

it feels good to have sex so harshly.

Love, death, kindness, filthiness, all same to me,

like desire shield itself when the love of newlyweds ensues.

As my present time stay, eventful glory, I want that too.

When that one touch arrives, I am yet to fall,

whispering, oh my god, that feels so fucking good.

Once arousing, I shout who wants oneself,

feeling I can't choose.

That drug I want, I can't let go,

does it have that timeless maze,

every time that flicker of lust heals my beating body,

every time those flicker of love makes my day,

making me wish for more.

The end is coming, showing that's the way,

I don't want an animal once again, but I'm.

Still, I do want the old ways,

that glimmer of quite a love,

that makes the body unknown, oneself overwhelmed.

by atif shahjad

Ringing the end

All way anyone can do.
It's just that truthful share.
When the water trunk gets full of poison,
I text her to make her mine.
As she wants to be mine,
her body did affect her to judge,
while I am a woman, stretching her greed,
she wants what is mine,
soft womanly charm, what she has seen,
she can't refuse,
I have all of it.
So I'm doing it,
waiting for the exact moment when she will walk in,
see me fucking her sister,
when her teeth will bite her own lips
as my present lover
tickling my nipple,
pushing her finger inside me,
eye catch the intruder standing at the door,
touching her, under her dress,
saying many things in her mind,
but waiting only for me in her repressed desire
as I got wetter by her watch what happing inside.

They did fuck

Him and her,
they both go far,
they are sinners,
they cause adultery in lust.
Between them,
he opens his lust,
she opens her naked beauty,
then it happens,
what wasn't meant to happen,
both are meant to be hung,
because both are broken stamps,
making their way to feeling numb.

by atif shahjad

Man is selling while you see the shadow

Took the time to fix

who are the junky,

anything I will do,

need my body?

Half what you will give,

get room to...

While you see the shadow,

the man is about to sell,

what he holds dear to you,

all that for a little glimmer of hard love,

which will make you forget,

what things do you put in your mouth,

who lost the bait,

to use me from behind, behind the set.

What would you like then,

or would you like another boy in his place?

He took me to his own place
when we love like ourselves.
Then he beat me, the incident happened.
I needed escape, so I run in distress.

Then we met,
her love took me to her boyfriend,
where we were torn apart
when I am between the two of them,
I have been able to adore differently,
in every corner of the touch,
everything went to me
when usually no one cares to see me.

—old branch of three

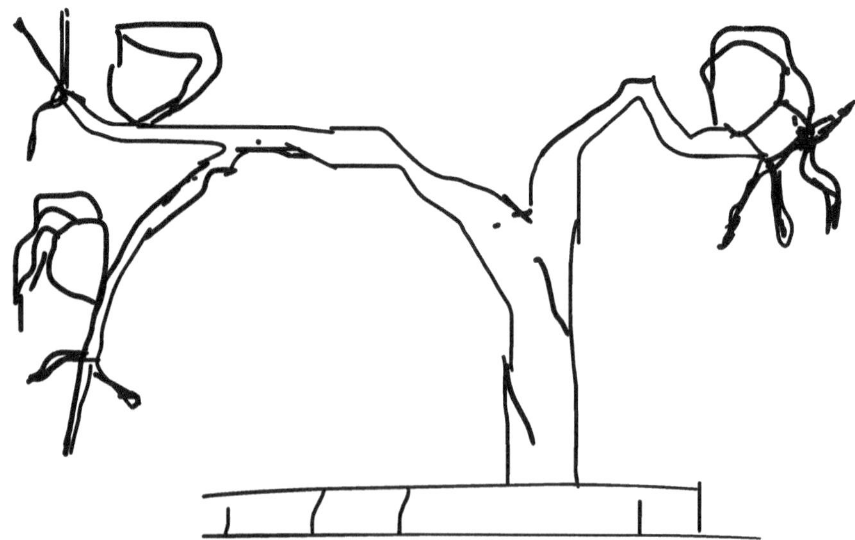

by atif shahjad

Queens tale

I did
agreed,
between two kingdoms
a bond was made,
as a king's son and warrior,
I followed my family's wish,
I married a princess,
whose family ensures an alliance.
For the first time, I saw her in my castle,
I have fallen in love, even though I didn't know what's love.
How can I,
all I know is the hounded glory of my royalty
while having everything.

But she became my wife.
On our wedding night,
laying within each other,
within her warmth,
it was the best thing
I ever experienced.
Then on, we talked, we listened,
we were there in each other pain.
I respected and trusted her wishes.
Years pass I never disrespect her,
hit her or blame her,
just loved her
as she is or was a queen of mine,
I'm sure she noticed.

But

an eventful war in our kingdom,

she was abducted.

When she was missing,

I have gone mad,

I got angry,

assembled an army,

cut myself strong,

fouth forward with my people

to spread the message,

while it costs double,

did spend half of the gold in tons.

Because I wanted my wife back,

I wanted her back,

at any cost.

She was in the hand of many wicked men.

They want her to be a story,

which will be the downfall of our history, our kingdom.

They wanted to brutalize our royal honor,

they want to rape and humiliate her,

but not death.

She will be sold as whore

who is my queen,

my queen,

and used as a coin breeder.

But there was a twist,

when she was captivated,

there was a man

by atif shahjad

who grew fond of her,
he has taken care of her
when she was abducted,
when they try to rape her
that man saves her,
shared his every burden,
and in return, she breathes for him.

Night after night,
that abductor was her protector.
And here,
I am the fool king,
going mad, raising an army, looking for her,
to save my lover,
my wife,
queen of this kingdom.

One night on the riverside,
that man and my wife sit next to each other,
they talked
about dream,
past life
which they left behind.
Then there was a moment appeared
when they kissed.
I wonder if she did not kiss back,
would that be the case
her protector couldn't have his cock between her lag
because he was there to protect her.

I wish it so many times
even an atheist like me prayed,
wished it to be true.
But I knew the truth
when laid down next to her,
when she told me yesterday that she loves me,
misconception—
She loved me.

That night, on the riverside,
they make love until a new dawn.
Every day she was there,
under everyone's nose
she made him stay in her bad
with the love that you give a person
who is your companion, lover, partner, or husband—
Now when I look at her body,
I see that man,
touching her tits,
thrashing his cock between her leg,
humping her in the arse.
Sorry, my lord, god, minister, adviser, and family,
all who are here to say goodbye to me,
for using all these wicked words.
Not at all my king.
Everyone said in reply.

Allegations against allegations,
I was gone there myself to save her.
But when I got there,

by atif shahjad

he was the one who stood in front of fifty men

to save her.

Those monsters want to humiliate her,

to walk naked,

fucked by nameless soldiers.

Before that happened,

I send a large amount of money for ransom

to give her back.

But within hours, I understand the story,

and attacked with my army,

And there was my wife,

who hiding behind that man,

who is the brother of their leader,

helped him to create this mess.

I was sewing my sword.

Every time a soldier cut me,

it did not hurt.

But it hurt

when she saw me in corner of her eyes,

but still, I was unseen.

It's like

for her,

I meant nothing

even if I imagine.

Because she is hiding behind his strength,

not calling my name to save her.

And at that moment,

my wife became whore in my mind.

Then the fight ended.
That man got wounded by saving her,
died within days.
I was injured too,
but for her, I remained as nothing to care for.
My friend and captain in my army,
tried his best to fix my body.
But what about my soul
that crushed when
I lost my queen
because I wanted to bring back my wife
not queen,
not lover,
my soul,
but she is already saved.

The night that man passed,
she cried.
I was her arm to drop tears,
I was there to comfort her hurt.
So I just sat still,
and lusted to hold her truly,
but I couldn't
because I wanted to be her glory,
not a story.

That night she talked, I listened.
Bit by bit,
she told me how their time passed,
what they did.

by atif shahjad

As her lover,
I have sat still to listen,
I laugh when she laughs,
I comforted her when she felt hurt,
I cried in my heart
when she describing love for him,
how they lay next to each other,
lived as one,
had each other in fun.
I listen to all of it,
not as a husband,
nor the king.
I just listened to her.
At least
she told me the truth
without fearing my judgment and rumor.
Thank you for that.

The queen lowered her head
with her eyes filled with tears
because the king looked at her and said this
like he won a war
but lost his purpose in life.
As soon as the king spoke it,
the whole hall began to hum.
Some words are heard,
the queen is a whore, she must die, she is not sincere, burn her,
outcast her from this kingdom.
Then kings cousin shouted,
and silence arrives in the king's hall.

Then king begins again ...
In the shadow of me,
she wasn't saved.
So I asked her,
does she wish to bury that man,
properly.
She said no like nothing happened.
Then I told my man to bury the dead.
And burn them
because it will dissolve the disease.
In the fight to save her,
I lost my forty men.
I am sorry for that.
All their family will be paid
with house and land.
But can I blame her for loving someone else?
I do not know.
She is my queen,
and always will be.
I thought my love was the truth,
which will be my faith,
but my queen picked a wild, wicked mad soldier to warm her,
and that is not okay.

After that burial,
we ride back home,
my queen got sick.
Then a maid said,
she was pregnant.

by atif shahjad

And you all can guess,

he is the son of the queen

and that man,

wicked brave man

who turns good by fucking a queen.

That moment,

I wanted to kill her,

I wanted to kill that child,

I wanted it so bad

that I brought hemlock from town villagers.

But I couldn't have the heart to do it.

She knew all of that,

I loved her,

I will punish her for unfaithfulness,

I wanted to,

but I did not,

and we arrived home,

in our kingdom.

Then the child is born.

The child you all are seeing,

Queen didn't want to tell the truth

because she wanted me to punish her, quietly,

not the child,

not her image as queen.

It will be a scandal,

and it is.

She begged me to tell everyone

he is my heir, my son.

She bagged,

she said she made a mistake,
to forgive her,
it will destroy her innocent image.
Even yesterday,
she came to my bad to warm me,
but I couldn't wake my flesh.

That moment felt longer than all the above.
My father was a king.
For him,
war and women are only hunger.
He fucked queens, ladies, whores.
My mother knew
but never did anything.
I knew.
Then my mother started fucking describe it.
Father and mother knew their sins.
As well mother never acted too confronting,
but my father acted
when he heard
my mother is sharing bad with someone,
telling everyone by conveying his misdeed,
he fucking killed him,
and torture my mother for years.
Because for him,
as long as he does the wrong,
it's right,
if anyone else does it,
it's a fucking war.

by atif shahjad

But I am not my father.
I made my peace.
For years, I have taken care of every one of you.
I was godly, a good king, a good husband, a good mentor, and a
good friend.
Before a king, I was a knight.
I always kept my honor.
I never bow down to anyone.
My army respects me
because they knew my grace, my devotion,
not power.

That's why I fought,
I wanted my wife and peace back.
But after nine years of ruling,
I lost many things.
My home is supposed to be my peace.
But did it stay that way?
My wife fucked, loved, laid in a bed with another man, betrayed me
and her king.
Now I harbor dysfunctional hate for the home I build.
Because the question raises,
did she ever love me at all?
If she did,
where is her faith when she fell for another man,
sharing what was promised to be mine?
But
I did love her,
and the worst part is,
I still do.

My love, I can't be with you anymore.
Then I will not remain a man at all.
You will be banished.
So take whatever money you like.
And before you beg,
at least, don't try because I love
—loved you, respect that.
In my eye,
you're my mistake,
you're my wife,
you're my dearest love, my queen.
If I was cruel, please forgive me.
Think of it as this,
maybe I would get a little peace.
But it will be better
if you don't see it unfold.
What has to be done to get this love,
you have an idea, don't you?
The way that I'm killing you, know this,
I just loved you, given everything,
even if you were raped,
I would tell my mind that you are a victim,
you loved me.
But you are my faith, the promise of a lifetime,
all faded.
I am not your husband anymore.
I wish you a happy life as a woman,
once who was my princess.

by atif shahjad

Buffalo love

Life is going far
while we are on the bus,
sitting on that narrow chair,
seeing how it will last ...
So you see,
little joy will not be love,
let's have sex
as she and he meant,
they need each other existence
when they sleep next to each other
in toxic attractiveness,
love,
sticking sentiment,
made their joy in bed, more needy and passionate,
every time
little to the edge,
sleeping together in a closed box
16 by 16 meters.
At night 4.41,
he will come to rape her,
she will fight, then give away,
what an odd roleplay
they quest to replay,
on the public washroom,
standing view in the wrong way,
still, their sex happens
between their real fantasy,
on library floor

between bookshelf.
It's done putting lasted want,
make morals hornet,
while it is what's wrong with killing the joy
when he wants every side more,
she just gives away
in one point
or another.
They remember the rule they sat,
do not wish for more,
then what happened in bed,
well well... They are doomed,
trouble in ton, in plain
he and she can't or would not be bound,
still inside those bones,
sex magazine should stop production for more, making them think
there is something more,
where in simple meaning, only desire is
you have to wish for what you want more is love and sex.

by atif shahjad

Snakeskin woman

Our skin tells us,

what is past,

our hearts tell us

what happened in previous heartbreak,

our faces tell us,

all along it's about you,

if care to obey.

Sometimes, our body does keep feeling

whom you share a condom with,

when we reach out to the evil blood

while having a period,

first time having sex,

in us, every drop of vigor

kept that priceless pride,

remember me, when once again,

your skin gets warm,

maybe I was your first, I will be the last of our kind.

Lollypop

Jonathon is a big shot.
In his pant, he puts on a dirty pot.
Kinda nasty,
but for girls he is tasty.
She meets, he she talks,
make love in a bed,
then towards areas,
his thing gets lost in her thing,
one and two began at the end,
in the morning, he is gone to a better trend.
Again tonight,
meets an older girl,
try his sinister seduces.
Sometimes when it's not working,
he shows his wild side.
For this, he is the Jonathon,
still kinda hasty,
tonight, they will be nasty.

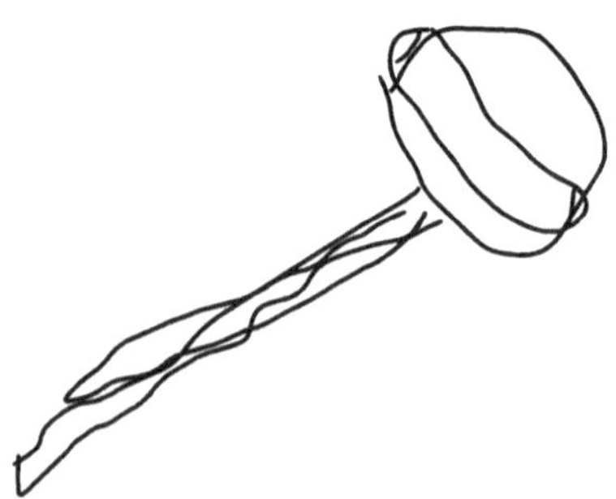

by atif shahjad

Tea with sugar

Halfway taking sugar isn't arousing skepticism,
is distance submission of lustful artwork,
not in younger life
when its alter ego tells the tale by saying,
I wanted more of her attention.

Sleepy-head

It's been a few days since we met.
Now it's all about sex owlet.

by atif shahjad

Unknown body

You have someone who loves you like crazy,

still, you want fuck somebody else?

Dude you did counseling.

You need to talk to your life partner,

then go to an orgy,

try something new

if you can imagine,

and there are quite a few.

Start with three

then go free,

where you will come to understand,

sharing isn't so bad.

In the wild dungeon,

you can be who you wanna be,

make no mistake.

Relations you have, make it real.

All fuck ups

have to be gone.

Moonlight waiting in your wager.

Don't fall for that perfection as a self-pleaser.

Wonder

between love and sex,

city inside your mind

that sleeps so unkindly.

Make your room in this love,

will of patience that stands

when you and your lover

goes no man's land so far.

Pagan whore

You have to let go of all wolves.
They are making noise for freedom.
Wicked Man will come,
kill the wolves.
They will humph you,
cut you for placeable joy,
semen will fill your arse.
Understand!
Would you?
My heart
still beats for you.
Be mine to humph.

If they kill,
you will bring me their puppy.
All I have is the wolves,
my decayed holes to be fucked.
I see fire,
that burns everything on my wedding day.
You bastard sold me
after you get bored.
Now you wish for me!
Burn in hell you pagan monster.

by atif shahjad

It's better to give the worst punchline

When can I see you butt naked?
What?
Her eyes asked,
are you mad serious to ask me that right now?
But with a laugh, maybe tonight, after nine.
See its faith,
no serious bullshit,
it's a date.
What a punchline—

Satisfied sound; porn and the real world

Ahh—this is a noise
where we understate that
I am tainted by you.
Mm-hm—as two people fucking each other or more
this expression becomes the rule of affection.
Oh, yeah—when it comes,
it becomes notable and perfect
like the gesture of last happiness, uh-huh with a simple backstabbing
face.
Hmmm—whatever you're doing in bed,
continue,
because after hmm satisfied sound conversation and nasty talk
happen, just the simple expression sound, mm-mm-mm, explaining.
Neither side goes up or down, where affected love comes to say, I'm
happy,
you know the starting point of sex and sound tricks.
And the universal sex satisfied comparability in sound everywhere,
always been an expression that moves in the sweet flow
when two people's lips meet and naked bodies change sweetness
into each other,
then it comes,
ah-ah-ah, I like it,
oh yeah, rub it,

by atif shahjad

mm-mm-mm, Mm-hm, love it,

and many odd ones like

Ahh.. Ah.. No-ahh.. Ah.. ah-oho.. nah.. Ha-ha.. Ahh.. Nah.. Hah-ha..

it feels so bad.

Does everyone make those sounds,

I say it like it's a faulty predicament.

Then the talk, don't cum inside

put on a condom,

what are you waiting for,

that's a woman sound,

and man's expression is, ahh, you like it, huh,

oh, hmm, oh yeah, mm-hm, put it in now, and a phrase like

you're beautiful and such.

Man's prostitutes calling

Now the name of a new profession for men can be heard,
sold out in exchange for money, selling themselves to hungry people.
However, many things individually have class
like for a young boy, the price is high,
muscular, somewhat handsome, fit middle-aged,
demand among their women,
or rather say,
the unfurling woman fantasy foreplay.
It's also the same as a woman who solids their pride,
needs saving from themselves by taking what can be yours.
Men and women desire the same, in that context.
That's why this profession repeatedly rejected and accepted
because there was a lot of gossip going on.
You know, man, you're not a coward, just like those chicks who sell
themselves.
So you say, so you do,
I will shoot the cannon to kill boredom on demand for money,
lay down as I unfold the cannon to go inside your wet lips between
your legs,
you dame mosquitos, squirt to die in the pleased demise of lust
because money is a prize, doing what must is a joy.
Also know it that meant fuel spears poking to be sold
because now there is a calling for men prostitutes in your hand,
young or old, cocky or bold, big or known for his ways of unfolding
is an attractive target to taste, but it is also a job
when he says, don't call me a prostitute or a man whore,
call me a gigolo.
Do any type of people will learn,

by atif shahjad

he, she and we are the same,

where the word does mean mystery,

yet they are just human, who just fucks and suck away at another

human want and serological performance,

sometimes in the category of prices, sometimes in someone's raw

naked lustful feat.

I wonder as a poet, what would be like to fuck a woman as a man

whore,

who call me by my many names

at a price to devour her bosom of innocent.

Hair and milk

If you escape through the back door, the milk stains will not
disappear by chance.
In the same way, falling on the floor ticks the body, while milk and
euphoria stain deep,
lips and mouth, the breast and nipples in the face of desire
do not mix with sex by sucking out the milk.
She goes, she arises, she poses, you see as well.
No matter what age you are, gender is welcome.
Naked flowers at the door of the gaze.
If you are deceived to distribute, you want happiness, to be a
combination of smell in your bristle love.
Because hair is wet with sweat, sweat comes on the skin, and
nipples on the face, cook on the later grace.
Injury to the penis in the vagina of the hips
quenched all the awful hunger, the semen mixes with the udder.
And it's the sickness that goes around when it comes to brittle,
at the border of time, this is not what you want, so come to the door
knob, arms around someone's chest, sit, always crammed with
excitement, having sex is the racists guest.

by atif shahjad

I want my body to be gentle to rough

There was no way back after the start.
That thrilling aristocratic time
I wanted, when my body was with him,
primitive animals used to play, the softness of love in this body,
unable to make an impression with a strong hand,
rough bindweed eye was his imaginary doing to me,
in every memorial lovemaking was a rough drawing.
His wanted lore of brusque on my body, made me want it more when
I sit on him,
I was kissing deeply, closed my eyes, bite his lips.
She was my attraction when I met him, her sari blouse with a skinny
waist, the new day was unbuttoned in her hand, with my hanging
high chest, what he craved out of me, seeing me that way,
I saw him take on a new look in the primitive game.
The people by the window did not see us.
Pretending to show these people from our side,
how he has taken me sexually, I was pleased to play along.
We used to do that
when the show was live, then our loved ones would come to find us.
But then neither of us got too drunk in this evil game,
in the eyes of both of us,
keeping quiet, tasting our delight,
we didn't spill secret story pictures
while I am obsessed with being rude and melancholy in this way for
no reason at all,
while during the clash of boats, he stopped with his footsteps and
kissed them all, he violates me sore.

When you had sex with me last night,
kissing me with dirty hands in a hungry grace,
I've been thinking about you ever since.
I can't think of anything but you,
how can I get that warm touch of the skin again?
The mind is restless, then your arrival happened.
I can't think of anything but you since yesterday.

—*sex aftermath*

by atif shahjad

This indistinct fantasy came true
when another companion was given consent,
when the hand found a knife, it cut through the hip,
the game of holding her breath in a plastic bag continued,
the play of dominance and subsequent sex,
quick intercourse with her, her hairy anus,
hands traction on her female pink skin,
rubbing, grabbing, and choking harshly
she taken,
who is insanely trying to stop him from breathing deeper inside
as he sees her, he takes her, rafts his hand around her neck
when the pleasure of his semen was coming to the genitals,
each push was bringing happiness to her deep body,
he quakes her body like a maniac.
This new extinction gave another form to sexual desire
while air ran out
as desire rises at fuck pitch,
she was allowed to breathe, right there,
at once her mouth filled with hard manhood, she will vomit on top,
or the heavy door on her backdoor will be let loose,
rushing with songs in a broken record, buzzing with infinite
complexity to feel submissive sex.
As she tries it, she became more satisfied with what that limit
you need to go, for that kind of pleasure.
Then she tries it, she gets on her knees, bent over like a tent
when his belt raft around her neck,
he says, don't you dare stop,
he puts it on,
then pulls it out,

the handcuffs on the hands put leather stains on the hands, color
red-brown,
yet his endless sex at every slap on her body does not stop,
at the end of this game, hunger burns
to give himself novelty.
Then she ties more ropes all over her body with her consent,
every floating word in the floating state, silently tells her buttocks,
inside her vagina, her tongue, shivering body tells her that there is
happiness,
surpassed this happiness, with your semen of joy squirting all over,
when he saw it, he pulled the hair back and bite her ears,
muttered as she begged him to bring everything to her everything,
his hand reaches the upper leg,
pull his weight on her, sucking her neck with those wet lips,
hooked into two bodies,
thus, she chants the chain like a song, experiencing
what I feel so wrong to be right...

—*indistinct happiness of the extinguished lamp*

by atif shahjad

How does it feel to cheat on someone?
Is that long-lost passion you want,
or the guilt that you have,
but wish to keep ...

—*feelings*

The desire for masculinity

We are males,

whose dissatisfied germs are divided into many desires and want,

confused spoiled vicious lust.

If It's good, It's good, it's all black.

On the red night of a cold morning,

lust blooms

when a stoner becomes whole with a flower,

they mate to ensure the desire for masculinity, sexist intercourse,

at least men do

Sometimes women too

when men become the unfortunate few.

Men, your identity is blindfolded,

whatever the world may say, this is the desire for the great truth,

your identity is the slave of desire, he knows you, going on and on about

how can I have sex, how can I feel?

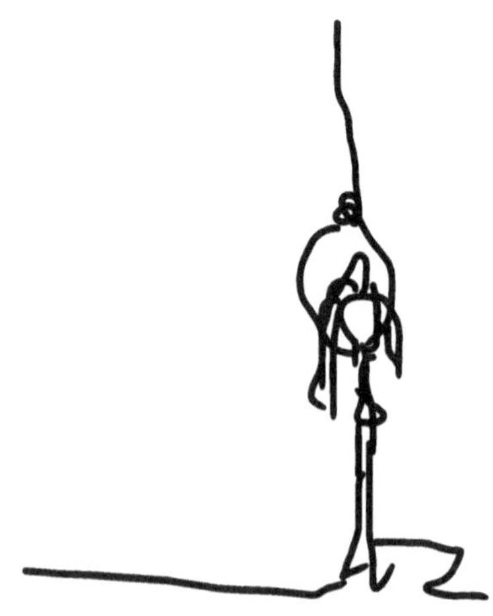

by atif shahjad

It's don't hurt

when released convicted sexual prevent

don't fetish his needs,

we all are the same,

we try to keep him quiet and sane,

his hand shackles himself until man-made ideas come.

It's don't bother us when massive misunderstandings are inflicted on

us broken,

the need to feed that dark desire,

it's just how it is displayed in the ongoing world.

Then what we need

doesn't exist anymore.

We don't have that compared relations and understanding, to open

ourselves to those action roleplay,

those who do have it,

they fail at it.

It's you that's aches in your solitude.

It's you who don't wish to change.

River flowers sinking in imaginary fragment

rather than cursing, exhibiting like a painting hanging in a gallery,

you don't know why

but still, carry it around in hope with it

you feel something, so what do you see,

things that you need, or indeed needed to keep.

—thorns tied to the custom

Under the pink

Age fourteen,

high school happened.

For herself, she was never loved,

at least she thinks it.

Prophet of coldest and bitchy,

everything front looks smooth and bitchy,

that she,

if you don't miss it.

She kissed a guy in a bathroom,

a girl saw it,

then rumor stated

she had sex with a stranger,

sucked him, fucked him, all the way in high school fantasies.

Otherwise, the jealous curiosity will not poke around

what it is that happened.

A few months later she sweetened it

and took it upon herself to self-absent in all weirdness.

Then one night in the backseat of a minivan,

she lost it.

Then she fucked sucked licked,

control is the mistress she out made herself,

but did she breathe the comfort,

who knew

with a rumor, a sweet girl wants to feel needed in sexual arousal,

trying to feel it

with a dick she did it,

but did she

or he felt it?

by atif shahjad

Boy age

That age is not to be forgotten.
I fell in love with girls
many times.
One day it turned into a physical caress,
then suddenly one day that body was with me,
whom I have not found, I have grown to fight,
yet in that boyhood, there was a fire of love,
but why is the dream floating in his body today?

Fairy tyrant

Then I was lost

when I saw him lying down,

slowly his body was getting lustful,

I was dreaming.

Then I realized that

I covered the spectacle mirror with the attraction of the stars,

I am included in the ordinance,

so I will not get a chance to eat his body,

love that around him

giggle like a supernova.

Yet he wakes up at night

when the naked bodies of so many people

standing in his window,

I wake up,

wake up my own womanly masculinity

in the far distance,

wanting to be the night in your story,

so put your lips in mine to love the aftertaste of my glorious beauty.

From then on, the night wakes up for him,

his greed gives my lustful body

a bag of peace,

when it doesn't work, happiness comes,

and I wish to stay in that dream.

by atif shahjad

She was long gone

Is it a wrong thing we are doing?

Hey, am I bothering you right now?

That is just a big empty spot in bed

where your husband usually sleeps.

It's like he is staring at me, mocking me, saying to me,

you can't be me, you're just a woman who fucks my wife's body to

satisfy, nothing more.

She is a troubled one, isn't she?

Seeing her acting this way,

the monk's wife says, what is it that got you up.

Don't you like us to have a good time?

No, not that.

it's just him, your husband.

—oh.

Simple-minded fellow, don't think about him.

He simply doesn't look at me that way.

And I don't need him

like I need you.

Why don't you come to bed,

I might have something to help you sleep.

She thinks she imagines about lover spiral.

Maybe, what can we do

or you can have all you want.

So she realized,

she was long gone for him.

Imagine that middle-aged woman

In the back room of the house, the young man took off my panties.
When his hand touched this middle age woman's buttocks,
I felt it pouring all out.
Then I did not let him take my whole body in my fine-build uniform,
but naked he got fast,
naked he wanted to fuck me,
he went down on me, licking my windows to my sand.
When I was disputing with myself, about everything, thinking about
him,
I was shoving his mouth deep inside me,
he takes it all the way, and I feel it.
Then he stands, rubs himself with my butt,
again, I felt aroused to the point, where I'm feeling the euphoria of
having sex
when every vein seemed to decapitate for that hot dick,
we started to fuck
by the window.
I felt so bad doing it,
while it felt so good that I am forgetting all of it
for a moment.
In this manner it goes on.
The seashore can be seen from the window, the people.
We were on the window side sunset table
while seeing outside, it made him scared, but I liked it.
So I kissed him, sucking his wet tongue, it tasted like coffee,
I looked at him and my nails scratched him a little
when his hand tickled and pulled my nipples, rubbing my tits
like it was his first time feeling them,

by atif shahjad

happiness was coming, yet for that time,

there was no intuition because everything else fades in the fun of

intercourse.

That thrilling young man gave me the joy to risk the day,

but my semen juice did not take him a man,

even though he fucked me well, I did get my satisfaction, so again I

shoved him down there until I came.

Because with age, comes the ugly side to taking what you want, so I

did.

And he was okay with it, wanting to fuck me again.

Nothing is there to loop

I am angry.
I want to hold your hand,
want sleep on your arm,
kiss you,
not on your lip,
other places.
I want to bath with you,
where your wet body will have love,
there your overpriced look will not be a judge,
all of me wants just a little of you,
that will be all I need.

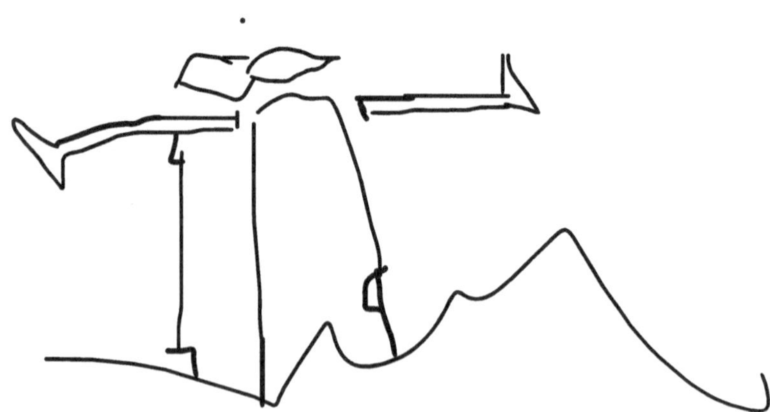

by atif shahjad

Magic Saga

What is this all about, don't tell me,

we've been here before,

there is a bad and a good lion,

there is a bad and a good wolf,

but their passion cross-references each other opposite

—how you define your love, sexual desire in your fantasy land.

Good lion and bad wolf can have a good life,

little children of their own,

bad time with some fresh spice.

But times move on to them,

they unknowingly broke each other,

then the debate in borderline unsatisfied need,

good lion says, all I did

is for us,

bad wolf says, all I did

is for you and this family,

not for me.

...rest unfolds.

Wolf cheats with old mate, lost love,

then find a new one.

A good lion falls for a nicer wolf, a stable wolf, who lives under

other's authority and rule,

then find his male pride love and sex view.

What an animal both of them,

so god, let them rot,

mistakenly just put their puppy love within a blank dot.

For a time being evolved around each,

lost magic, now nowhere to run,

but let me tell this story another peach.

Bad lions and good wolves also have a perfect life,

little playthings of their own,

rock and roll of their saxophone.

But the magic in wonderland,

which made them less like each other,

nevertheless, all things considered

time moves ahead to break them,

they unknowingly broke each other.

Here lion abuse and say, all this your fault.

When what's the fault, no one knows.

Wolf says I can't take it anymore.

You broke me first.

...all that's left, becomes a mystery.

Then the lion charmer goes wonder in many holes where he can fit

in,

one after another

until the similar one like before,

he doesn't rest to snore.

Loner wolves find comfort in the home,

where love can roam, where she can love

whomever she bones.

Then after a time,

she gives herself another chance like before,

just like a hey tree, let's make me free.

So they go round and round to jump at the same shore.

In middle what's needed,

for each other nothing stays left.

by atif shahjad

Lover touch softly kept,
round and round pouring themself each one into the ground,
magic lost, yet kept themself locked,
without looking for their best.

That's why I know,
we've been here before,
letting go harder than after
than before.
The only way I see
don't be so open book to peak,
keep a little mystery,
find the best me
where you can see yourself loving the best of me.

Glasshouse

I didn't want proper,
so I gave him leads.
I just wanted to get laid,
fuck for a while,
without my beautiful body,
my nice breast,
and my excellent taste in things,
forgetting everything,
just fuck.
But with it,
did it move along,
which got me on this downplay,
affection with each selfless phase
that stayed.
But I did cum, actively fantasying about you.
Before that moment,
I started rubbing myself around that guy's lag,
quietly moaning,
on one hand, I am squeezing my left tits,
other hand giving hand-job,
feeling him, asking him to close his eye,
yet
imaginary you there beside me
in fantasy, everything is about you,
rushing me,
putting into a limitless encounter with you,
where you're using me in a way
as a woman none other you've ever seen,

by atif shahjad

every time you kiss and love me inside out,

I am making a happy sound,

looking at your eyes.

And suddenly I cum in my real-world rubbing on his lag,

and that guy was weirdly satisfied.

Because whatever I see in view,

I mean to see you,

I ache for your touch,

so long I long your storm

where I feel good only by you—

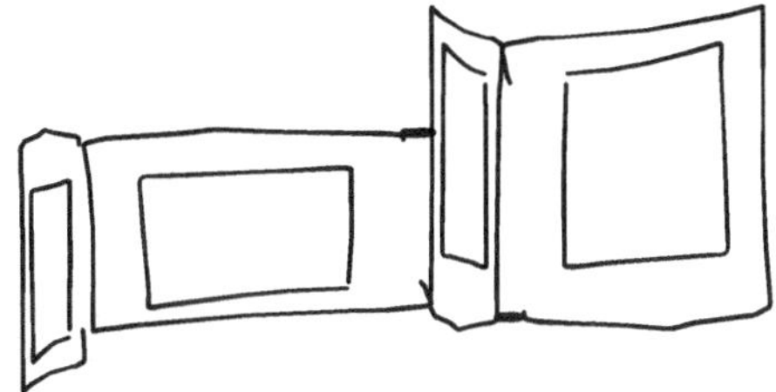

Sex masked freewill

Can't it be true
we not wanting anything
like friends with sex benefits,
whenever we need,
can be used as a needed kit.
Like buying a burger in a food corner will be our greatest joy,
having sex in a cheap motel room will be the greatest mistake
because the wall is too thin.
But we will do it together,
happy or sad,
what remained unchanged,
then what we will be
enough to describe as human beings—

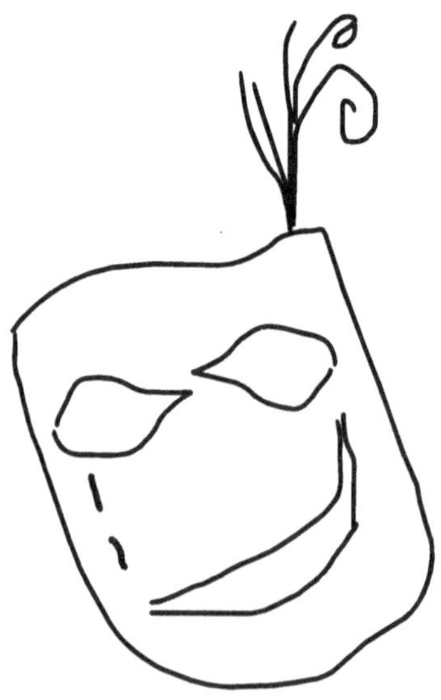

by atif shahjad

I am careful about what I wish for,
I know what my worth is.
That's why I cheat on everything to have it all,
not a little bit to lose it all.

—*before all went to shit*

He says hi
where are my keys staying inside
because it's getting hard again
when resolving issues don't serve us well.
Brutal
but the way it is
they all make moments go by,
then nest became the lost lie,
in bed, where sweaty bedsheets cry,
we lay down close
to cool off our burning fire,
remaining undenied.

—lost in your apartment

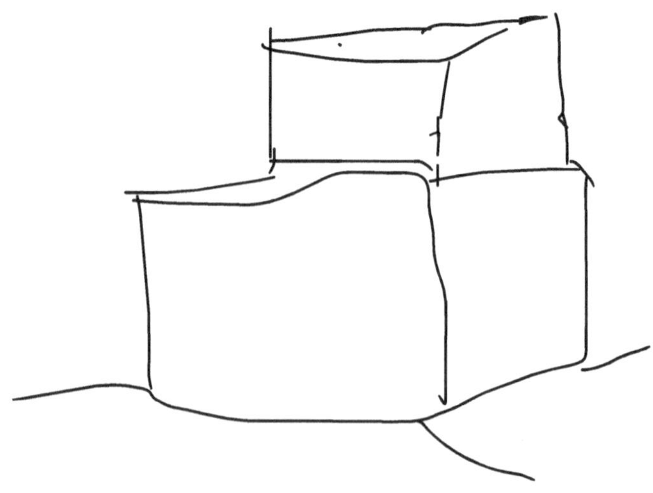

by atif shahjad

An unwanted affair

Time was the thing that made me miserable,

but what's more, your distance surprise and excuse

brought real distance between us.

Every time I put you first,

you run far.

Every time I love you,

you just have my body

nothing else you need from me.

Sometimes at night, it hurts,

I cry myself to sleep,

yet you never look my way

So I push you away.

Then I just need to belong somewhere

as that person came into my life,

I started to like it

when he fucks me in bed,

when he tears up my body,

how he cared for me,

love me like you once did,

I felt alive.

Still, you did not see me,

you pushed away,

nevertheless worried

as much as my guilt.

You don't even look at my eye,

you left me all alone,

you fucked up.

Yet

we had conversations like a stranger.

We talked,

I acted out,

but you never suspected.

Maybe you loved me more than me.

Return for you, the truth was never

more incomplete

who only believe I am your good lover,

even when I don't get your love back,

the way that I need to.

Because that is not a relationship

when the love you give,

in return, you get nothing,

not even a single passionate kiss.

Because that is true love

when the love you give

it comes back to you,

haunts to the deaths of hell.

So don't worry,

until you die, I will be there for you.

But the new

was the only thing now I want.

Then somehow you knew, years later.

Then I told you, you told me, how can you do this to me?

Maybe you should have asked that years ago.

Now it's too late.

by atif shahjad

Truth did not hide in the dark, no more.
At a perfect time, we sort to be
who we were meant to be.
I left you alone,
and still remember your smile of regret
because I was the one who didn't wait long for your love.
Maybe you had affair like me too.
Just didn't tell me.
Maybe your all mystery love
and distance is the way you stayed faithful.

But I never wanted that.
I wanted you.
I wanted more for me, more for this body, more satisfaction and
closeness.
Still
to the end,
somehow you were
the bad one.
But why can't I blame myself for leaving you, why was it that
I got off so easy, I ask it many times,
but the answer remains the same.
If not,
maybe then reality will have me different
or less sad in my happy life.

Had nothing

Broken people have the thrill to give

as I saw I had fallen for, a married woman with a paranoia issue.

And I was the messed-up guy, with his imaginary guilt,

but my kindness and romance were her wanted thing

she never had.

As we got close, we did spend time, every way we had each other

when I was inside her, wet lips on my desire,

I was relaxed and drowning in rain,

waiting for a sunny day to come.

But at some point, that wasn't enough anymore,

being there

after every orgasm, her face plays the guilty trials.

Without this kinky sexual arousal,

nothing was there,

But she ended it a year later because I was her mistake,

for a year?

But I have known the truth,

the past love never dies in another man's bed,

it stays asleep

until you called upon it,

broken people know it well, as I do,

where sex in a dungeon was an early coming appearance

as our feelings,

until that mature life take over, when fixing us is the only way,

but it had to be done our way.

Yet today, when I remember our time,

she came into my dream when the love of my life sleeps in my arms.

by atif shahjad

Live one day in her shoes

It wasn't her, all the bad things you do,
it was yours when your hand cut their wings
because you like her as a dog,
fuck from behind as a slave,
saying you are my whore.

But if she does the same thing to you,
will you like that
because it's that mind saying around the closed wall,
that wasn't you like.

The drug you will get addicted

There she is, knowing all the stops and choices,
if she willingly explores the thing
you like her to be,
how fun it will be.
So give her that, test her skin but do not put your rules with your
cook's brain.

If she gets the choice of freedom,
and still, want your ugly side to make her a bitch,
then you win the play
without being a prude snitch
of your manly pride.
So being open isn't so bad
when the lover spiral doesn't get out of hand,
she became the drug you will get addicted to, come back over and
over
searching for more.
So let her be that
because I know in my gut,
I would like that very much.

by atif shahjad

What did you tell?

That window got narrow,

but I told you,

all the mistakes I do

that does not mean I don't love you.

Monkey see,

donkey do,

neither was my doing

when I saw his soft hand,

grabbing you, when you're liking it,

when your issue made you fall

for unaccepted person

that I never imagine,

still, this heart loves you like always does.

About the author

Writer Atif Shahjad is a modernist, artist, editor, designer, and social protester, who is devoted to making an impact through his writing and changing people's points of view. Some call him a rebellious thinker, some a truth-seeker, some an audialistic lecturer. His principles and beliefs as a human being are somewhat unique.

'I believe in god, but not in religion. What is the real truth of the religion, culture, and faith that differentiates society and humans? Creation is by no means one of belief and opinion. There is a view of everything, whether it is by discrimination or as a vagabond.

- Atif Shahjad

Born on 31 July 2000 in a small village in Bangladesh. His written manuscripts resemble realistic own opinions. Writer Atif essentially focuses on every category of writing sharing his journey, lessons, and mistakes along the paths of manhood and love, compassion, other people's points of view, and story texture. The significance of this type of writing is found in the postmodernism style, modern writing, and storytelling sense. This is the idea of his spark, and the agenda he obeys as a writer.

For example, he wrote a true story-based poem Red Petticoat which has been widely criticized at all levels for the writer's storytelling presentation of society's ideas and enigmas faced by the reader, which we blindly ignore.

This Bangladeshi writer published his first writing at the age of 14. From then on, his journey started. Many of his manuscripts have been published in newspapers and domestic magazines. He also has many activities as a drawing artist. Needless to say, it is a bit difficult to get an idea of what he is obsessed with as an artist.

Writer's other books

Word Clitoris Awake, 1st edition (Dusty Blue, Vol - 1), Sweetbitter Tastes of My 19 Years. 2nd edition, (Dusty Blue, Vol - 1), All of Me (Dusty Blue, Vol - 2), Subtitle of that story; I do not give a fuck, I, you, he, she, we, and this ruthless world

Poet's dream, Filthy Shades of Love: Draft 17.53, OSTOROSA; All the River Stream in Life's Poetry, Conversation, Conversation II (Vol - 2), Opu and his nameless writer friend (Dusty Blue, Vol - 3), The sunflower of my secret love (Dusty Blue, Vol - 4)

Upcoming books

Slut

In the end, it's all about sex and dominance

Understanding healing